OFFGRID PLANNING
Workbook

OFFGRID
HOMESTEAD
FAM

OFFGRIDHOMESTEADFAM.COM

Printed in the United States of America.

For more information, or to book an event, contact :

zani@offgridhomesteadfam.com

http://www.offgridhomesteadfam.com

Cover design by Yasir Nadeem

Formatted by Femigraphix

Edited by Abby Hale

ISBN - Paperback: 979-8-218-31934-2

First Edition: February 2024

TABLE OF CONTENTS

INTRODUCTION

Welcome to the Offgrid Planning Workbook, your essential companion on the path to a self-sufficient and harmonious life away from the grid. As you embark on this journey, it's crucial to understand what "offgrid" truly means. It's not merely about disconnecting from public utilities; it's a profound lifestyle choice—a deliberate step toward independence, sustainability, and a deeper connection with nature.

Why do people choose to go offgrid? For some, it's a longing for the serenity of rural landscapes, the desire to reduce their environmental footprint, or the dream of self-reliance. Others seek freedom from the constraints of urban living and the relentless pace of modern society. Whatever your motivation, going offgrid represents a commitment to a simpler, more intentional life.

Yet, this path is not without its challenges. From harsh weather conditions to potential isolation, there are real dangers to consider. This is precisely why crafting a meticulous and airtight plan is paramount. You're not just building a home; you're designing an entire lifestyle. The Offgrid Planning Workbook is here to guide you through this intricate process, helping you clarify your vision, identify your priorities, and chart a course toward your offgrid dream.

Within these pages, you'll find invaluable worksheets, resources, and expert insights that will empower you to create a holistic offgrid strategy. From budgeting and location finding to property acquisition and sustainable living practices, every aspect of your offgrid adventure is covered. It's your comprehensive roadmap to a life of self-sufficiency and fulfillment.

In this journey towards offgrid living, every step you take is crucial, and the assignments within this workbook are designed to be your stepping stones. It's important to emphasize that the full benefit of the "Offgrid Planning Workbook" can only be realized when all of its exercises and tasks are completed. These assignments are meticulously crafted to guide you through the multifaceted process of offgrid planning, covering every essential aspect from conceptualization to actualization. They are not just theoretical exercises but practical tools that will shape your understanding, refine your goals, and crystallize your strategies. By diligently working through each task, you'll build a robust and comprehensive plan tailored to your specific needs and circumstances. This thoroughness ensures that you're not just dreaming of an offgrid life but actively constructing a viable, sustainable path to achieve it. Remember, each completed assignment brings you one step closer to turning your offgrid aspirations into reality.

So, let's get started. Your offgrid journey begins here, and with the Offgrid Planning Workbook as your trusted companion, you're equipped to turn your dream into a thriving reality.

MY REASONS WORKSHEET

Instructions: Complete this worksheet at the beginning of your offgrid planning journey. This assignment will assist you in articulating why you are interested in this lifestyle and will be the beginning of clarifying your vision. Please note that some of your answers may change upon the completion of this process.

What has drawn you to exploring offgrid life?

_____

_____

_____

What do you dislike about your current life?

_____

_____

_____

How will moving offgrid improve your life?

_____

_____

_____

How do you envision your offgrid life?

_____

_____

_____

What are your hesitations or fears about moving offgrid?

_____

_____

_____

What can you do to alleviate your fears/hesitations?

_____

_____

_____

How are you going to fund setting up your offgrid life?

_____

_____

_____

What are some amenities that you can't live without?

_____

_____

_____

What is your desired & realistic timeframe to be offgrid full-time?

_____

_____

_____

What do you have to do to obtain the funds by your desired timeframe?

_____

_____

_____

CLARIFYING YOUR VISION & THE POWER OF VISION BOARDS IN REALIZING DREAMS

Every great accomplishment begins with a vision — a clear, focused idea of what one desires to achieve. Clarifying this vision is paramount because it serves as a beacon, guiding decisions and actions and propelling individuals forward even amidst challenges. It's akin to setting a destination in one's internal GPS; without knowing the endpoint, the journey can become aimless, haphazard, and lack direction.

A vision board, in this context, is a tangible manifestation of that destination. By creating a collage of images, quotes, and affirmations that resonate with one's dreams, individuals effectively map out their aspirations. This visualization tool serves multiple purposes. First, it offers a daily reminder of what one is working towards, ensuring that goals remain top of mind. Second, by engaging in the act of curating and assembling a board, individuals immerse themselves in the emotions, sensations, and feelings associated with their dreams, effectively solidifying their commitment.

Moreover, there's a psychological dimension to this. The brain works remarkably well with visual stimuli. When it constantly sees images related to one's goals, it begins to recognize them as attainable realities rather than distant dreams. This shift in perception, bolstered by the repeated exposure from a vision board, can subconsciously steer one's actions and decisions towards making those dreams a reality.

In essence, clarifying one's vision and creating a vision board work in tandem to act as both the compass and the map for life's journey. They ensure that dreams are not just fleeting thoughts but are consistently nurtured, pursued, and eventually realized.

VISION CLARIFICATION ASSIGNMENT

This assignment will assist you in bringing your dream out of your mind , onto your vision board, and into fruition. It will also serve as a reminder of what you are working towards.

What is the minimum amount of acres that would be ideal?

_____

_____

_____

What will your land look like?

_____

_____

_____

Where will your property be located?

_____

_____

_____

What type of housing will you be starting with?

_____

_____

_____

What type of forever home will you have? Describe what it will look like, how may bedrooms, bathrooms, etc.

_____

_____

_____

How will you heat/cool your temporary and/or forever home?

_____

_____

_____

What will your bathroom facilities look like, and how will you dispose of your waste?

_____

_____

_____

What would your garden look like? (i.e., outdoor, hydroponics, greenhouse, walipini)

_____

_____

_____

What type of storage will you have?

_____

_____

_____

Will you have firearms on your property? If so, what type?

_____

_____

_____

What type of vehicle will you have?

_____

_____

_____

Are there any luxury items that you wish to have (pool, sauna etc.)?

_____

_____

_____

What type of animals will you have, and what is your timeframe for purchasing?

TYPE OF ANIMAL	TIMEFRAME AFTER MOVING

What kind of structure will you have for your animals, supplies, & feed?

_____

_____

_____

What other things will you have on your property?

_____

_____

_____

How will you make money offgrid?

_____

_____

_____

Are there any specific events that you are looking forward to once you have moved off-grid?

_____

_____

_____

Are there any other goals you have for your property?

_____

_____

_____

VISION BOARD INSTRUCTIONS

Creating a vision board is extremely important for your journey! There has been a lot of research proving the effectiveness of vision boards. They are a representation of our positive and ideal future. It helps you have a clear idea of what you are working towards. They help you understand what you want to manifest.

Find Images and Words for the Vision Board.

- Use the Vision Clarification Tool as your guide.
- Google pictures of the answers you provided in the assignment.
- Find the picture that most beautifully fits your vision of each object.
- Print out each image or add to a Word document to change the sizes and then print.
- Even if you don't have a printer, add all of the photos to one document or save individual pictures, then email it to your local Office Depot, UPS store or go to the library to print it.

Create a Basic Structure for the Vision Board.

- This can be done in many ways, and you can be as creative as you like.
- You can tape or pin all of the pictures directly onto a wall.
- Or you can purchase a poster board to adhere all of your pictures to.

Assemble the Vision Board.

- Get creative in the order or patterns that you use to add your pictures.
- You may want to add some words that appeal to you, or for things that you can't find images for, like Generational Wealth, Passive Income, Independently Wealthy etc.

Embellish! Make Your Vision Board Fun and Visually Appealing.

- Do you want to add a little glitter or boarders?
- You can get supplies for making a scrap book to add extra character and bling to your board.

Display Your Board.

- Once your vision board is complete, hang it on the wall where you will see it regularly. Think—your office, bedroom, or living room.
- It's important to create a vision board, but equally important to see it regularly.

Use Your Vision Board as a Road Map.

- Making the vision board is just the beginning!
- Now it's time to use it as a guide and road map into your new future.
- There are so many ways you can do this, such as:

  - Create an action plan for your goals (and then take action!)

  - Review your board as you create it, whether it's your to-do list for the day or week

  - Journal about the goals depicted on the board

  - Practice visioning exercises (closing your eyes and imagining the achievement of your goal)

HERE ARE SOME EXAMPLES OF HOW YOU CAN MAKE YOUR OWN VISION BOARD!

NOTES

THE DELICATE BALANCE OF OFFGRID LIVING: ESSENTIALS, SOLAR POWER, AND THE ART OF DOWNSIZING

As one embarks on the journey to offgrid living, a critical step in the process is discernment — determining what is truly essential and what can be left behind. This introspection isn't just about physical possessions; it's about understanding the nature of offgrid living and the distinct differences between on-grid and offgrid lifestyles.

Solar electricity, for instance, stands as a prime example of these differences. While the sun offers a renewable and sustainable energy source, harnessing its power for daily use presents a distinct set of challenges. Solar power systems have their limitations based on capacity, sunlight availability, and energy storage.

Unlike the seemingly endless supply from the grid, solar energy necessitates a heightened awareness of consumption. Common household appliances, which on the grid might be used without a second thought, can quickly deplete solar reserves. High-energy devices such as microwaves, hair dryers, electric kettles, or large entertainment systems might become luxuries, or may need to be used judiciously. Therefore, before investing in solar panels and battery storage, one must critically evaluate their energy needs, often leading to a redefinition of 'essential' appliances.

Offgrid living, often perceived as a monolithic concept, actually encompasses a diverse array of lifestyles. Each offgrid homestead is as unique as its inhabitants, varying widely in its level of modern conveniences and amenities. This spectrum ranges from the most basic, rustic existence to sophisticated setups that rival the comfort of on-grid homes, each tailored to the desires and priorities of the individual.

At one end of the spectrum lies the minimalist approach. Here, individuals opt for a life that is stripped down to the bare essentials. These offgridders often forgo electricity altogether, relying on traditional methods for light and warmth, such as candles, oil lamps, and wood stoves. They embrace a lifestyle that is deeply connected to the rhythms of nature, often involving manual labor for daily tasks. This form of offgrid living requires not only a profound commitment to simplicity but also a resilience and skill set that harkens back to earlier times.

Moving along the spectrum, we encounter offgridders who incorporate a modest level of electricity into their lives. This middle ground typically involves a small solar setup or a wind turbine, just enough to power essential electronics like lights, a phone, and perhaps a laptop. It's a lifestyle that balances the rustic charm of offgrid living with a nod to modern convenience, offering a more accessible entry point for those transitioning from a fully grid-dependent life.

Then, at the opposite end of the spectrum, we find a version of offgrid living that could easily be mistaken for a high-end, on-grid lifestyle. Here, large solar arrays, possibly complemented by wind or hydro power, feed sizeable battery banks, providing ample electricity for a range of appliances and luxuries. These setups can support everything from refrigerators and washing machines to home entertainment systems, offering a level of comfort and convenience that challenges common perceptions of offgrid living. While this approach requires significant financial investment and technical expertise, it represents the pinnacle of self-sufficient luxury.

Each of these variations of offgrid living speaks to a different set of values, priorities, and resources, illustrating that there is no one-size-fits-all approach. Whether it's the raw authenticity of minimalism, the balanced pragmatism of moderate electricity use, or the comfort of a fully-powered offgrid home, each represents a unique interpretation of what it means to live off the grid.

This reevaluation extends beyond just electricity. The shift to offgrid living often corresponds with moving to a smaller, more sustainable living space. This transition inherently calls for a downsizing of possessions. Items that once held importance in the on-grid world might find little to no utility in the offgrid environment. For instance, a collection of kitchen gadgets might be rendered superfluous in a simplified cooking setup. Or a vast wardrobe might need to be pared down to functional, durable clothing suitable for the new environment.

But this process of discernment and downsizing isn't about sacrifice; it's about clarity. It's about understanding the true essence of living, distilling life to its core necessities, and finding joy in simplicity. As many seasoned offgridders will attest, shedding the excess often leads to a richer, more fulfilling experience. By consciously choosing what to bring into this new life, one paves the way for a journey that is not only sustainable but also deeply resonant with one's values and aspirations.

WHAT CAN YOU LIVE WITHOUT?
COMFORT , CONVENIENCE & AMENITIES

COMFORT/ CONVENI-ENCE ITEMS	CAN YOU LIVE WITHOUT IT?	HOW LONG CAN YOU LIVE WITHOUT IT?	NOTES & COMMENTS
Electricity			
Running Water			
Septic			
Cell Service			
Wi-Fi			
Hot water			
Showers			
Heat			
Air conditioning			
Refrigerator			
Freezer			
Oven			
Microwave			
Toaster Oven			
Toaster			
Built-in Dishwasher			
Portable Dishwasher			
Washing Machine			
Dryer			

COMFORT/ CONVENI- ENCE ITEMS	CAN YOU LIVE WITHOUT IT?	HOW LONG CAN YOU LIVE WITHOUT IT?	NOTES & COMMENTS
Coffee Maker			
Vacuum			
Blender			
Food Processor			
Instant Pot			
Rice Cooker			
Slow Cooker			
Stand Mixer			
Juicer			
Waffle Iron			
Bread Machine			
Ice Cream Maker			
Yogurt Maker			
Coffee Grinder			
Popcorn Machine			
Panini Maker			
Deep Fryer			
Food Dehydrator			
Water Purifier			
Sewing Machine			
Iron			

DOWNSIZING WORKSHEET

Instructions: Use this worksheet as a guide to help downsize your possessions in preparation for transitioning to an offgrid lifestyle. Take your time to go through each category and make thoughtful decisions about which items to keep, donate, sell, or discard. Remember to prioritize functionality, versatility, and long-term value when considering what to keep. Use additional sheets if needed.

Category: Clothing and Personal Items

1. Assess your wardrobe:

   - Take inventory of your clothing, shoes, and accessories.
   - Determine which items are essential and suited for your offgrid lifestyle.
   - Consider the durability, versatility, and climate appropriateness of each piece.
   - Make piles of what you will keep, donate, sell, or discard.

2. Personal hygiene and grooming items:

   - Evaluate your toiletries, skincare products, and grooming tools.
   - Discard expired or unused items.
   - Consider sustainable and minimalistic alternatives.
   - Make piles of what you will keep, donate, sell, or discard.

Category: Kitchen and Dining

1. Cookware and utensils:

   - Assess your kitchen supplies, including pots, pans, and utensils.
   - Keep versatile and essential items that suit your cooking needs.
   - Consider downsizing duplicates or items you rarely use.
   - Make piles of what you will keep, donate, sell, or discard.

2. Dishware and glassware:

   - Evaluate your collection of plates, bowls, glasses, and mugs.
   - Keep enough for your family's needs while minimizing excess.

- Consider lightweight and durable options for offgrid use.
- Make piles of what you will keep, donate, sell, or discard.

Category: Electronics and Entertainment

1. Electronics:

   - Assess your electronics, including computers, televisions, and gadgets.
   - Consider the energy consumption and necessity of each device.
   - Opt for energy-efficient options that align with your offgrid goals.
   - Make piles of what you will keep, donate, sell, or discard.

2. Books, CDs, and DVDs:

   - Evaluate your physical media collection.
   - Consider digitizing or donating items to reduce clutter.
   - Opt for e-books, digital music, and online streaming services.
   - Make piles of what you will keep, donate, sell, or discard.

Category: Miscellaneous

1. Furniture and home decor:

   - Assess your furniture pieces and home decor items.
   - Prioritize functionality, comfort, and space optimization.
   - Consider multi-functional or modular furniture options.
   - Make piles of what you will keep, donate, sell, or discard.

2. Sentimental items:

   - Assess sentimental possessions such as photographs, heirlooms, or mementos.
   - Keep items that hold significant personal value and memories.
   - Consider digitizing or creating a memory box for keepsakes.
   - Make piles of what you will keep, donate, sell, or discard.

By systematically evaluating each category and making intentional decisions about your possessions, you can downsize effectively and create a more streamlined and clutter-free living environment. Remember to approach this process with mindfulness and an understanding of the unique needs and constraints of your offgrid lifestyle.

NOTES

FINANCIAL FOUNDATIONS FOR OFFGRID ASPIRATIONS: ASSESSING FINANCES, DEBT, AND ASSETS

Embarking on an offgrid journey requires a comprehensive evaluation of your current financial status, including an in-depth look at your finances, debts, and assets. This scrutiny is crucial in determining the viability and scale of your offgrid project and, potentially, in shaping the strategies you might need to employ, such as liquidating assets or securing financing.

Begin by assessing your financial health. This means taking a hard look at your income streams, savings, and any existing debts. Understanding where you stand financially will help you gauge how much you can comfortably invest in your offgrid venture without jeopardizing your economic stability. It's about striking a balance between your offgrid aspirations and your current financial obligations.

For many, transitioning to an offgrid lifestyle may involve liquidating assets. This could include selling property, downsizing possessions, or even tapping into investments. The decision to liquidate assets should be approached with a strategic mindset, weighing the long-term benefits of offgrid living against the short-term sacrifices. This process can significantly bolster your budget for the offgrid setup but requires careful consideration to ensure that you're not undermining your future financial security.

Additionally, the evaluation of your creditworthiness becomes paramount, especially if there's a need for financing. Whether it's for purchasing land, investing in solar panels, or building a sustainable home, most large-scale endeavors may require a loan. A good credit score can be a gateway to favorable loan terms and lower interest rates and it can make a substantial difference in the feasibility of your project. If your credit score is not where it needs to be, it might be prudent to dedicate time to improving it before embarking on the offgrid transition.

Beyond these financial considerations, it's equally important to assess your current career and income potential in the context of offgrid living. An offgrid lifestyle might necessitate career changes, especially if your current job is location-dependent or incompatible with offgrid living. Identifying potential career switches or additional training and skills required to secure a high-paying remote job or start a business is a critical step. This may include exploring online courses, attending workshops, or networking in your desired industry to prepare for a smooth transition.

Brainstorming potential income streams from the land itself can also be a rewarding endeavor. This could involve agricultural activities like farming or permaculture, offering retreats or workshops, or even developing artisanal products. When considering these options, it's essential to align them with your interests and skills. Passion often drives success, and if you enjoy what you're doing, it will reflect in the quality of your output and the sustainability of your business model. Additionally, consider what resources — both physical and educational — you may need to invest in to make these ventures successful.

The journey to offgrid living requires a holistic approach that encompasses both financial readiness and career adaptability. By thoroughly assessing your financial situation, considering career transitions, and exploring potential land-based income streams, you create a robust framework for a sustainable and fulfilling offgrid life. This comprehensive planning ensures that your transition is not only a leap towards independence but also a strategically sound financial decision.

FINANCIAL EVALUATION AND PLANNING WORKSHEET

The Offgrid Financial Evaluation and Planning Worksheet is a valuable tool to assess your current financial situation, set goals, and develop a plan to achieve your offgrid homestead dreams.

Current Financial Assessment

1. Calculate your average monthly income after taxes:

    Monthly income: $_____

2. Calculate your average monthly expenses (include housing, utilities, groceries, transportation, etc.):

    Monthly expenses: $_____

3. Determine your monthly savings or surplus (income minus expenses):

    Monthly savings/surplus: $_____

4. Evaluate your current savings and assets:

    Savings account: $_____

    Investments: $_____

    Other assets: $_____

5. What is your current credit score _____

    Is your current credit score an acceptable place to obtain financing

    _____

    Is there anything that you can do to increase your credit score if needed:

    _____

_____

_____

Financial Goals and Homestead Development

1. Before doing any research, how much money do you think you need to buy land and build infrastructure? $ _____

2. Determine the timeframe in which you would like to achieve your financial goals:

_____

Short-term (1-3 years) Medium-term (3-5 years) Long-term (5+ years)

Exploring Income Opportunities

1. Assess your current career and income potential:

Is there room for growth or advancement in your current field?

_____

_____

_____

Are there opportunities for salary increases or promotions?

_____

_____

_____

Are you considering a career switch to increase your income potential?

_____

_____

_____

2. Identify potential career switches or additional training/skills required to secure a high-paying remote job or start a business. List new career paths or industries you are interested in:

_____

_____

_____

Determine the training or certifications needed for these potential career paths:

_____

_____

_____

Estimate the time and financial investment required to acquired these skills:

_____

_____

_____

3. Brainstorm potential income streams from the land. Include things that you would enjoy and what resources it may take to become successful:

Farming/gardening:

_____

_____

_____

Livestock raising:

_____

_____

_____

Value-added products (e.g., artisanal goods, homemade preserves):

_____

_____

_____

Agritourism (e.g., farm stays, workshops):

_____

_____

_____

Other ideas:

_____

_____

_____

_____

_____

_____

_____

_____

_____

_____

Developing a Financial Plan

1. Assess your current financial situation:

    Determine your monthly savings potential: $ _____

    Is there anything that you can do to decrease your expenses:

    _____

    _____

    _____

    Identify any outstanding debts or financial obligations:

    _____

    _____

    _____

2. Set financial targets:

    Determine the amount of money you need to save each month to achieve your goals:

    _____

    _____

    _____

    Identify strategies to increase your savings or reduce expenses:

    _____

    _____

    _____

3. Create a timeline for achieving financial milestones:

Break down the steps required to achieve your financial goals:

_____

_____

_____

Set milestones for each step and assign estimated timelines:

_____

_____

_____

4. Evaluate potential funding sources:

Savings or emergency funds:

_____

_____

_____

Loans or financing options (if needed):

_____

_____

_____

Grants or subsidies for agricultural initiatives:

_____

_____

5. Regularly review and update your financial plan:

How will you monitor progress towards your goals:

_____

_____

_____

How will you adjust strategies as needed:

_____

_____

_____

How will you seek professional financial advice if necessary:

_____

_____

_____

Remember, this worksheet is designed to help you evaluate your current financial standing and develop a plan for achieving your offgrid dreams. Customize it to fit your specific circumstances and goals. Regularly reassess and update your financial plan as you progress. Seek professional advice when needed. With careful planning and execution, you can turn your offgrid aspirations into a reality. Good luck on your financial journey!

NOTES

TAILORING YOUR OFFGRID ELECTRICITY SOLUTION: BALANCING NEEDS, ENVIRONMENT, AND FINANCES

When embarking on an offgrid lifestyle, one of the most crucial decisions involves selecting an appropriate electricity source. This choice is not just about personal preference but also about assessing the feasibility of various options in diverse environments and understanding your specific energy needs.

Evaluating Your Energy Needs

The first step is to calculate your current electricity usage, which lays the foundation for deciding your offgrid power system's size and capacity. Examining your electric bill to understand your monthly kWh usage provides a baseline. However, it's equally important to consider the energy consumption of individual appliances. Items like refrigerators, heaters, and air conditioners are typically high-energy users. Understanding the specifics of your consumption can help determine the capacity needed for your offgrid system.

Exploring Offgrid Electricity Options

Solar panels are a popular choice for offgrid living due to their relative ease of use and decreasing costs. They are most effective in areas with abundant sunshine but can be supplemented with batteries for night use or cloudy days. The scalability of solar systems allows for gradual expansion as needs grow or finances allow.

In areas with consistent wind, turbines can be an excellent power source. Wind energy can complement solar systems, providing power during cloudy or stormy weather when solar output is reduced. If your property has access to flowing water, a small hydroelectric generator can be a reliable and constant energy source. These systems are particularly effective in regions with less sunlight but require access to a suitable water source.

Generators powered by gasoline, diesel, or propane are commonly used for offgrid power. While they can be efficient, they also require a steady fuel supply and maintenance. They're often used as backup options in conjunction with renewable sources. Combining two or more of these systems can provide a more reliable and consistent energy supply. For instance, solar and wind power can complement each other, with wind energy providing power during the night or on cloudy days when solar panels are less effective.

Building an offgrid power system often requires a significant initial investment, especially for renewable energy setups like solar or wind. Starting with a smaller system that meets your basic needs and expanding over time can be a more financially viable approach. This phased strategy allows you to manage costs while gradually increasing your system's capacity.

Choosing the right offgrid electricity option requires a careful balance between your personal energy needs, the environmental conditions of your chosen location, and your financial capacity. By thoroughly assessing your current energy usage and understanding the strengths and limitations of each power source, you can design an electricity solution that is both practical for your offgrid lifestyle and adaptable to future changes.

ELECTRICITY PLANNING WORKSHEET

Instructions: Use this worksheet to evaluate your current energy usage and plan for an offgrid energy source for your homestead. Assess each section and record your energy needs, usage, and goals. This will help you make informed decisions about the type of energy system that best suits your requirements.

List all the electrical appliances and devices used in your home. (this may require a separate sheet depending on how many appliances you use). Then, estimate the average daily usage hours for each item.

Use this formula to estimate an appliance's energy use:

(Wattage × Hours Used Per Day) ÷ 1000 = Daily Kilowatt-hour (kWh) consumption

1 kilowatt (kW) = 1,000 Watts

APPLIANCE	WATTAGE	HOURS USED	DAILY kWh

Assess the solar potential of your location by considering the average daily sunlight hours and shading issues.

_____

_____

_____

Evaluate the wind potential of your location by researching average wind speeds and patterns.

_____

_____

_____

Determine the size and type of wind turbine suitable for your energy needs.

_____

_____

_____

Assess any zoning restrictions or noise considerations related to wind turbine installation.

_____

_____

_____

Assess if you have access to a water source with sufficient flow and drop for hydroelectric power.

_____

_____

_____

Determine the appropriate size and type of hydro turbine based on your energy requirements.

_____

Consider the environmental impact and any permits or regulations related to hydroelectric systems.

_____

_____

_____

Evaluate the availability and feasibility of each energy source (solar, wind, hydro, or a hybrid system in your chosen location. Consider factors like climate, available space, and local regulations.

_____

_____

_____

Determine the energy storage capacity required, such as batteries or other storage solutions.

_____

_____

_____

Calculate the desired battery bank size based on your daily energy consumption and expected backup needs.

_____

_____

_____

Assess the charging and discharging rates and the overall efficiency of the energy storage system.

_____

_____

_____

Estimate the initial cost of the offgrid energy system components, including installation and maintenance.

_____

_____

Research available incentives, grants, or tax credits that can help offset the costs.

_____

_____

Assess the maintenance requirements of the offgrid energy system, including routine inspections and potential repairs.

_____

_____

Research the recommended maintenance tasks, intervals, and associated costs.

_____

_____

Evaluate your ability and resources to handle the required maintenance or consider professional assistance.

_____

_____

Set a realistic timeline for implementing the offgrid energy system of your choice. Consider factors such as budget constraints, availability of equipment, and installation requirements.

_____

_____

_____

Note: This worksheet provides a general framework for evaluating energy usage and planning for an offgrid energy source. It is important to conduct thorough research, consult professionals when necessary, and adapt the information to your specific circumstances and location.

NOTES

CHOOSING THE RIGHT OFFGRID WASTE DISPOSAL SYSTEM: BALANCING NEEDS, ENVIRONMENT, AND REGULATIONS

When living offgrid, managing waste efficiently and responsibly is a key component of a sustainable lifestyle. The decision on how to dispose of waste is influenced by individual needs, the environment, and local regulations. It's crucial to choose a system that aligns with these factors to ensure both environmental protection and compliance with legal standards.

1. Composting Toilets:

For human waste, composting toilets are a popular choice among offgridders. They convert waste into compost that can be used to enrich the soil, reducing water usage and preventing pollution of local water sources. These toilets are ideal for areas without sewage systems but require proper maintenance to ensure health and safety. It's important to check local regulations as some areas have specific rules regarding the use of composting toilets and the disposal of compost.

2. Septic Systems:

In more permanent offgrid setups, especially those with access to water, a septic system can be a viable option. Septic systems treat wastewater naturally and release the treated water back into the ground. However, they require significant upfront investment and space for installation. Regular maintenance is crucial to prevent environmental contamination. Local building codes often dictate the type of septic system allowed, so compliance is key.

3. Incineration Toilets:

Incineration toilets, which burn waste to ash, are an effective solution for waste disposal in areas where composting is not feasible or preferred. They are efficient, leave behind minimal residue, and reduce the volume of waste significantly. However, they require energy to operate and can be costly.

4. Graywater Systems:

These systems filter and repurpose wastewater for irrigation, reducing water consumption. The feasibility of a graywater system depends on the quality of the water and local regulations, as some areas have strict guidelines on graywater use.

5. Solid Waste Disposal:

Solid waste, such as packaging, food scraps, and other non-biodegradable materials, needs careful consideration. Reducing consumption and reusing materials can significantly decrease the amount of solid waste. For the waste that cannot be avoided, check local regulations for disposal or recycling options. In remote areas, you might need to transport this waste to proper disposal or recycling facilities.

6. Recycling and Upcycling:

Implementing a robust recycling system is essential. Segregating waste and recycling materials like glass, metal, and certain plastics can substantially reduce your environmental impact. Upcycling, or creatively repurposing waste materials, can also be an effective way to minimize waste.

Choosing an offgrid waste disposal system requires a holistic approach, considering your lifestyle needs, environmental impact, and adherence to local regulations. It's about finding a balance between practicality and sustainability, ensuring that your offgrid life remains in harmony with nature while respecting legal boundaries. By carefully considering your options and planning your waste management strategy, you can maintain a clean, healthy, and sustainable offgrid environment.

WASTE DISPOSAL PLANNING WORKSHEET

Instructions:

Use this worksheet to plan for waste disposal on your offgrid homestead. Assess each section and record your waste management needs, potential methods, and infrastructure requirements. This will help you make informed decisions about the most suitable waste disposal system for your property.

Research outhouses, composting toilets, incinerating toilets, or septic systems designed for offgrid use.

_____

_____

_____

Research local requirements and evaluate options for waste management in your chosen area.

_____

_____

_____

Research local recycling facilities, composting methods, and waste collection services.

_____

_____

_____

Assess the possibilities for treating and reusing graywater from sinks, showers, and laundry if legal.

_____

_____

_____

Research graywater filtration and treatment systems suitable for offgrid use.

_____

_____

Determine the infrastructure requirements for storing and distributing treated graywater for irrigation or non-potable uses.

_____

_____

Evaluate options for managing blackwater from toilets and other waste sources.

_____

_____

Determine the infrastructure requirements for proper handling, treatment, and disposal of blackwater.

_____

_____

Consider the potential risks to groundwater, surface water, and soil quality and implement appropriate measures.

_____

_____

Determine the infrastructure needed for each waste management method, including storage containers, compost bins, treatment systems, or septic tanks.

_____

_____

_____

Research suitable equipment, their costs, and any necessary permits or approvals.

_____

_____

_____

Evaluate the feasibility of implementing and maintaining the required infrastructure on your property.

_____

_____

_____

Estimate the initial cost of implementing the chosen waste disposal systems and infrastructure.

_____

_____

_____

Research available incentives, grants, or rebates that can help offset the costs.

_____

_____

Consider ongoing maintenance and operational expenses, such as composting materials or septic system pumping. Assess recommended maintenance tasks, intervals, and associated costs.

_____

_____

_____

Evaluate your ability and resources to handle the required maintenance or consider professional assistance.

_____

_____

_____

Consider safety measures for handling and storing waste, such as proper labeling, containment, or protective equipment.

_____

_____

_____

Set a realistic timeline for implementing the chosen waste management systems and infrastructure. Consider factors such as budget constraints, availability of equipment, and seasonal variations in waste generation.

_____

_____

_____

Divide the project into manageable phases if necessary.

Note: This worksheet provides a general framework for planning offgrid waste disposal. It is important to conduct thorough research, consult professionals when necessary, and comply with local regulations and best practices. Adapt the information to your specific circumstances and location.

NOTES

THE LIFELINE OF YOUR HOMESTEAD — SECURING A RELIABLE AND SUSTAINABLE WATER SOURCE

Water is the essence of life, a fundamental need that becomes even more critical when you step into the world of offgrid living. In an offgrid homestead, water is not just a convenience; it is a vital resource that plays a central role in nearly every aspect of daily living. From personal hygiene to food production, the availability of a reliable and sustainable water source can make the difference between a thriving homestead and one that struggles to survive.

Consider the numerous ways water integrates into homestead life. For personal use, water is essential for drinking, cooking, bathing, and laundry. In addition to household needs, if your homestead includes a garden or small-scale agriculture, irrigation becomes a significant water consumer. Livestock, too, require a consistent and clean water supply. Then there's the need for water in various homesteading activities, such as canning, brewing, or even artisanal crafts.

When planning for water on an offgrid homestead, there are several options, each with its unique benefits and considerations. The most common and sustainable method is rainwater harvesting, which involves collecting and storing rainwater for later use. This method is highly dependent on local climate patterns and requires a good catchment area, such as a roof, along with storage solutions like cisterns or barrels.

For those with access to a natural water source, such as a stream, river, or spring, direct water access can be an excellent solution. However, it's crucial to ensure the water quality is safe for use and to understand the legal implications and water rights in your region. In some areas, the use of natural water sources is heavily regulated.

Wells are another viable option for many offgridders. Drilling a well can provide a steady, reliable source of water, although it requires an initial investment and ongoing maintenance. The feasibility of a well largely depends on the groundwater levels and quality in your area.

In more arid climates or locations where other water sources are not viable, hauling in water might be necessary. Hauling water is a method often employed by many new offgridders as they establish their homestead, but it's important to recognize that this approach is not a sustainable long-term solution. Relying on external sources for your water supply means that you lack control over a vital resource, leading to potential challenges and uncertainties in your offgrid lifestyle.

No matter the source, water conservation should be a key principle in your offgrid water strategy. Techniques such as drip irrigation, graywater systems, and water-efficient appliances can significantly reduce water usage. Being mindful of water use not only ensures the sustainability of your homestead but also aligns with the broader ethos of offgrid living — living in harmony with the natural environment.

In summary, securing a reliable and sustainable water source is one of the most critical aspects of setting up an offgrid homestead. The right water strategy provides a backbone for your daily needs, agricultural endeavors, and overall sustainability of your homestead. Careful consideration, planning, and adaptation to your environment are key to ensuring that this vital resource supports and nurtures your offgrid dream.

WATER SOURCE PLANNING WORKSHEET

Instructions:

Use this worksheet to plan for offgrid water sources for your homestead. Assess each section and record your water needs, potential sources, and infrastructure requirements. This will help you make informed decisions about the type of water system that best suits your needs.

List all the water requirements for your household, including drinking, cooking, cleaning, bathing, irrigation, and livestock.

_____

_____

_____

Estimate the average daily water consumption in gallons or liters.

_____

_____

_____

Assess the availability and suitability of potential on-site water sources such as wells, springs, rainwater harvesting, or surface water.

_____

_____

_____

Evaluate the quantity, quality, and reliability of each water source.

_____

_____

Consider factors like annual rainfall, groundwater levels, and legal regulations.

_____

_____

_____

Determine the feasibility of drilling a well on your property by assessing the geological conditions and water table depth.

_____

_____

_____

Research local drilling regulations, permits, and recommended well construction practices.

_____

_____

_____

Estimate the cost of drilling, equipment, and ongoing maintenance.

_____

_____

_____

Evaluate the potential for collecting and storing rainwater by considering the average rainfall in your area and the roof catchment area.

_____

_____

_____

Determine the appropriate rainwater storage capacity based on your water needs.

_____

_____

_____

Research rainwater collection systems, including gutters, downspouts, filters, and storage tanks.

_____

_____

_____

Evaluate the need for water treatment or filtration to ensure the water's safety after lab testing of each water source.

_____

_____

_____

Research suitable water storage options like tanks, cisterns, or reservoirs.

_____

_____

_____

Assess the need for water treatment systems such as filters, UV sterilizers, or water purification tablets.

_____

_____

_____

Evaluate the plumbing infrastructure needed to distribute water throughout your property, including pipes, faucets, and irrigation systems.

_____

_____

_____

Assess the distance from the water source to your living areas and any potential challenges in installing the plumbing network.

_____

_____

_____

Estimate the initial cost of implementing the chosen water sources and infrastructure, including drilling, equipment, storage, and treatment systems.

_____

_____

_____

Research available incentives, grants, or rebates that can help offset the costs.

_____

_____

_____

Assess the maintenance requirements of the water sources, storage systems, and treatment equipment.

_____

_____

Research recommended maintenance tasks, intervals, and associated costs.

_____

_____

Evaluate your ability and resources to handle the required maintenance or consider professional assistance.

_____

_____

_____

Set a realistic timeline for implementing the chosen water sources and infrastructure.

_____

_____

_____

Consider factors such as budget constraints, availability of equipment, and seasonal variations in water availability.

_____

_____

_____

What will be your temporary water source while setting up your permanent system?

_____

_____

_____

Divide the project into manageable phases if necessary.

Note: This worksheet provides a general framework for planning offgrid water sources. It is important to conduct thorough research, consult professionals when necessary, and adapt the information to your specific circumstances and location.

NOTES

NAVIGATING OFFGRID HOUSING OPTIONS: FROM READY-MADE TO SELF-BUILT HOMES

The spectrum of offgrid housing options ranges from purchasing a fully equipped offgrid property to converting an existing on-grid home, or even starting from scratch on raw land. Each path offers its unique challenges and rewards, and the best choice depends on your preferences, skills, and budget.

For those seeking a more turnkey solution, buying a fully set up offgrid property can be ideal. These homes come with essential offgrid systems like solar power, water collection, and waste management already in place. This option saves the time and effort needed to install these systems and allows for a smoother transition to offgrid living. However, fully equipped offgrid properties may come with a higher price tag and less customization.

Another option is to purchase a traditional on-grid property and convert it for offgrid living. This process involves disconnecting from utility services and installing independent power, water, and waste systems. It offers more flexibility in terms of location and property type but requires a significant amount of work and knowledge about offgrid systems.

Starting with raw land offers the most customization but also poses the greatest challenge. You have the freedom to design and build a home that perfectly matches your vision and needs. This process, however, involves extensive planning, from securing permits to constructing and installing all necessary offgrid systems. It often requires the most time and financial investment.

If you choose to build on raw land, temporary housing becomes a crucial aspect to consider. Options like living in an RV, a tiny home, or even a yurt can provide a comfortable dwelling while constructing your permanent home. These temporary solutions offer a practical way to live on-site and oversee the building process.

The variety of offgrid homes is vast, ranging from traditional log cabins and modern eco-houses to innovative options like Earthships, yurts, and tiny homes. Each type comes with its unique aesthetic, efficiency, and environmental impact. For example, Earthships are built with natural and recycled materials and are known for their sustainability and energy efficiency. Yurts offer a more nomadic and minimalistic living style, while tiny homes strike a balance between compact living and modern conveniences.

Choosing your offgrid home is a deeply personal decision that sets the tone for your new lifestyle. Whether it's buying a ready-made offgrid house, converting an existing property, or building from the ground up, each option requires careful consideration of your long-term goals, lifestyle preferences, and practical constraints. By understanding the spectrum of choices and their respective implications, you can select a path that aligns with your vision of offgrid living.

HOUSING PLANNING WORKSHEET

Instructions: Use this worksheet to help you consider important factors when planning the construction of your offgrid home. Take your time to assess each aspect and make notes on your preferences and requirements. Remember to customize the list based on your specific needs and circumstances.

Will I be able to build my forever home immediately?

_____

_____

_____

Will I be living on the property while my home is being built?

_____

_____

_____

TEMPORARY HOUSING

If I need temporary housing, what is the best option for me?

_____

_____

_____

How will I heat and cool my temporary housing?

_____

_____

How will I dispose of my waste while living in temporary housing?

_____

_____

_____

FOREVER HOME

What does my dream home look like?

_____

_____

_____

Number of bedrooms?

_____

_____

_____

Number of bathrooms?

_____

_____

_____

What is the square footage?

_____

_____

Does it include thermal mass?

How will waste be managed?

What heat source will be used?

What cooling source will be utilized?

What type of storage will I incorporate?

Will there be any specific features or amenities that are important to my offgrid lifestyle?

_____

_____

_____

NOTES

THE BEDROCK OF OFFGRID PLANNING: BUDGETING WITH PRECISION AND REALISM

Embarking on the path to offgrid living is an exhilarating endeavor, filled with dreams of freedom, self-sufficiency, and harmony with nature. However, beneath the romance of this journey lies a pragmatic foundation: budgeting. Establishing a comprehensive and realistic budget during the initial planning stages is not just advisable—it's imperative.

Moving offgrid involves numerous expenses, some of which might not be immediately apparent. From land acquisition to infrastructure setup, from renewable energy systems to water and waste management, every facet of the transition requires careful financial consideration. Without a well-thought-out budget, one runs the risk of encountering unexpected expenses, leading to financial strains or, worse, unfinished projects.

But how does one ensure the accuracy and realism of their budget? The key lies in proactive research—specifically, obtaining precise quotes for each aspect of the transition. While online resources and anecdotal references can provide ballpark figures, they often fail to capture the nuances and specificities of individual projects. Local pricing variations, unique challenges presented by a particular plot of land, and even fluctuations in material costs can significantly influence the final price tag.

By reaching out to professionals, contractors, and service providers to obtain detailed quotes, one can paint a realistic picture of the financial landscape ahead. This process also offers the added benefit of fostering relationships with local experts who can provide invaluable insights and recommendations tailored to one's specific needs.

Moreover, a budget anchored in actual quotes becomes a dynamic tool in the planning process. It allows for prioritization, revealing which projects are feasible in the short term and which might need to be deferred or reimagined. It provides clarity, ensures that funds are allocated effectively, and prevents the pitfalls of overextension.

In essence, while the spirit of offgrid living is rooted in freedom and self-reliance, its successful realization hinges on meticulous planning. And at the heart of this planning lies a robust, realistic budget, serving as both a guide and safeguard on the journey towards sustainable living.

INSTRUCTIONS FOR THE INITIAL BUDGET PLANNING WORKSHEET

This exercise is a crucial step in your journey towards a sustainable offgrid lifestyle. Before diving into the worksheet, ensure you have completed the assessment of your current financial situation, including income, debts, assets, and potential income streams. This information will be essential in guiding your budget allocations.

Purpose of the Worksheet:

The goal of this worksheet is to help you gather realistic quotes and estimates for various aspects of your offgrid transition, allowing you to understand and plan how much money you will need. By the end of this exercise, you should have a clearer picture of how far your current financial resources can stretch and where you might need to adjust your plans or expectations.

1. Research and Quote Gathering:

   - For each category, conduct thorough research to understand the typical costs associated. Reach out to professionals and service providers for detailed quotes. Remember, the more accurate your estimates, the more reliable your budget plan will be.

2. Inputting Estimates:

   - Input the quotes or estimated costs next to the respective category. If you receive a range of costs, use the higher estimate to ensure you have a buffer in your budget.

3. Total Budget Requirement:

   - Sum up the costs to get a total budget requirement. This will give you an overview of the total financial commitment needed for your offgrid transition.

4. Financial Assessment Comparison:

   - Compare this total with the assessment of your current finances. Determine how much money you can allocate to each category based on your available resources.

5. Adjustment and Prioritization:

   - If you find that your financial resources do not cover all expenses, this is the time to prioritize. Decide which elements of your offgrid setup are essential and which can be deferred, adjusted, or downsized.

7. Contingency Plan:

   - Allocate a portion of your budget for unexpected expenses. Offgrid transitions often encounter unforeseen costs, and having a contingency fund is crucial.

8. Regular Review and Update:

   - As you progress in your offgrid planning, regularly revisit and update this worksheet. Quotes may change, or you may find alternative solutions that are more cost-effective.

Remember, this worksheet is a living document, pivotal to your offgrid planning process. The diligence and accuracy you apply here will greatly influence the success and feasibility of your transition to offgrid living. Take your time, be thorough, and let this worksheet be your financial compass guiding you towards a sustainable future.

INITIAL BUDGET PLANNING WORKSHEET

LAND

EXPENSE	LOW ESTIMATE	HIGH ESTIMATE	NOTES
LAND PURCHASE			
SURVEY COSTS			
TITLE INSURANCE			
ENVIRONMENTAL TESTING			
SOIL TESTING			
PERC TESTING			
CLOSING COSTS			
CLEARING LAND			
GRAVEL DRIVEWAY			
UNEXPECTED			
TOTAL:			

HOUSING

EXPENSE	LOW ESTIMATE	HIGH ESTIMATE	NOTES
STRUCTURE			
FOUNDATION			
PERMITTING & FEES			
ELECTRICAL WIRING			
PLUMBING			
FURNITURE			
APPLIANCES			
HEATING			
COOLING			
LABOR			
BATHROOM			
KITCHEN			
ADDITIONAL			
ADDITIONAL			
UNEXPECTED			
TOTAL:			

WATER

EXPENSE	LOW ESTIMATE	HIGH ESTIMATE	NOTES
PERMITTING & FEES			
WELL DRILLING			
PRICE PER FOOT:			
AVG. WELL DEPTHS:			
WELL PUMP & INSTALLATION			
WELL HOUSE STRUCTURE & PIPING AROUND PROPERTY			
CISTERN/IBC TOTES			
CISTERN/TOTE PUMP			
GUTTERS			
PRESSURE TANK			
WATER TESTING			
WATER FILTER			
UNEXPECTED			
TOTAL:			

ELECTRICITY

EXPENSE	LOW ESTIMATE	HIGH ESTIMATE	NOTES
PERMITTING & FEES			
PANELS			
PANEL STAND			
BATTERIES			
CHARGE CONTROLLERS			
INVERTER			
WIRING			
BREAKER			
GROUND RODS			
OUTLETS			
DISCONNECT			
CONTROL PANELS			
INSTALLATION			
GENERATORS			
ADDITIONAL MATERIALS			
HYDROMETER			
MULTIMETER			
BATTERY CHARGER/DES-ULFATOR			
UNEXPECTED			
TOTAL:			

SEWAGE

EXPENSE	LOW ESTIMATE	HIGH ESTIMATE	NOTES
PERMITTING & FEES			
CONTRACTOR FOR IN-STALLATION			
IF NOT USING A CONTRACTOR			
TOOLS			
DIGGING HOLE			
SEPTIC TANKS			
PVC & DRAINIAGE			
GRAVEL			
ADDITIONAL MATERIALS			
UNEXPECTED			
TOTAL:			

STORAGE

EXPENSE	PRICE	NOTES
PERMITTING & FEES		
FOUNDATION		
STRUCTURE		
MATERIALS		
SHELVING		
UNEXPECTED		
TOTAL:		

GARDEN

EXPENSE	PRICE	NOTES
GREENHOUSE		
MATERIALS		
TOOLS		
TOTAL:		

SECURITY

EXPENSE	PRICE	NOTES
FENCING		
GATES		
CAMERAS		
LIGHTS		
LOCKS		
DOG		
FIREARMS		
TOTAL:		

ANIMALS

EXPENSE	PRICE	NOTES
BARN		
FENCING		
FEED BARRELS		
LIVESTOCK		
ADDITIONAL SUPPLIES		
TOTAL:		

OPTIONAL ITEMS

THIS IS WHERE YOU ADD ANY ADDITIONAL OUTBUILDINGS, LUXURY OR NEEDED ITEMS AND ANYTHING ELSE ON YOUR VISION BOARD.

EXPENSE	LOW ESTIMATE	HIGH ESTIMATE	NOTES
FARM VEHICLE			
TRACTOR			
PROPANE TANKS			
WIFI			
CELL SIGNAL BOOSTER			
TOTAL:			

NOTES

INSTRUCTIONS FOR THE FINAL BUDGET PLANNING WORKSHEET

Congratulations on reaching the stage of completing the Final Budget Worksheet in your "Offgrid Planning Workbook." This step is crucial as it builds upon the initial budget planning and your comprehensive understanding of both your financial capacity and the realistic costs associated with transitioning to offgrid living.

Purpose of the Worksheet

The Final Budget Worksheet is designed to help you allocate your available funds to different aspects of your offgrid project based on the quotes you've gathered and your financial assessment. This exercise will enable you to create a detailed and actionable financial plan for your offgrid transition.

1. Review Initial Budget Worksheet:

   - Start by reviewing the estimates and quotes you collected in the Initial Budget Planning Worksheet. Pay close attention to any changes or updates in the pricing.

2. Update Available Funds:

   - Reassess your available funds, considering any changes in your financial situation since the initial assessment. Include savings, income, liquidated assets, and potential loans.

3. Allocate Funds to Categories:

   - Begin allocating your available funds to each category (land, construction, solar system, etc.). Start with essential categories that are critical to your offgrid setup.

4. Balancing Act:

   - Ensure that your allocations do not exceed your available funds. This might require revisiting your priorities and making adjustments to ensure that critical aspects of your project are funded.

5. Consider Cost-Saving Alternatives:

   - If you find yourself over budget in certain areas, look for cost-saving alternatives or cheaper solutions without compromising on quality or necessity.

6. Detailing and Documentation:

- Document the allocated amount next to each category, along with any notes on how you plan to manage that budget (e.g., phased approach, DIY elements, etc.).

7. Contingency Allocation:

- Set aside a contingency fund (around 10-20% of the total budget) for unexpected expenses or price fluctuations.

8. Final Review and Adjustment:

- Conduct a final review of your budget allocations. Ensure that each essential category is adequately funded and that the overall budget aligns with your financial capabilities.

9. Plan for Monitoring and Reassessment:

- Establish a plan for monitoring expenses as you progress in your offgrid project. Regularly reassess and adjust your budget as needed based on actual spending and any changes in your financial situation.

10. Documenting Future Financial Planning:

- Include a section for future financial planning, considering ongoing costs such as maintenance, property taxes, and other recurring expenses in your offgrid life.

By methodically allocating your funds in the Final Budget Worksheet, you're laying down a financial roadmap for your offgrid journey. This structured approach ensures that your transition is grounded in financial realism, enhancing the likelihood of a smooth and successful transition to your new sustainable lifestyle. Remember, flexibility and regular reassessment are key components of effective budget management, especially in a dynamic endeavor like offgrid living.

LAND

EXPENSE	PRICE	NOTES
LAND PURCHASE		
SURVEY COSTS		
TITLE INSURANCE		
ENVIRONMENTAL TESTING		
SOIL TESTING		
PERC TEST		
CLOSING COSTS		
CLEARING LAND		
GRAVEL DRIVEWAY		
UNEXPECTED		
TOTAL:		

HOUSING

EXPENSE	PRICE	NOTES
STRUCTURE		
FOUNDATION		
PERMITTING & FEES		
ELECTRICAL WIRING		
PLUMBING		
FURNITURE		
APPLIANCES		
HEATING		
COOLING		
LABOR		
BATHROOM		
KITCHEN		
INSULATION		
ADDITIONAL		
UNEXPECTED		
TOTAL:		

WATER (WELL, WATER CATCHMENT, SPRING, STREAM, DELIVERY AND/OR HAULING)

EXPENSE	PRICE	NOTES
PERMITTING & FEES		
WELL DRILLING PRICE PER FOOT: AVG. WELL DEPTHS:		
WELL PUMP & INSTALLATION		
WELL HOUSE STRUCTURE & PIPING AROUND PROPERTY		
CISTERN/IBC TOTES		
ADDITIONAL PUMP		
GUTTERS		
PRESSURE TANK		
WATER TESTING		
WATER FILTER		
UNEXPECTED		
TOTAL:		

ELECTRICITY (SOLAR, WIND, HYDRO-ELECTRIC)

EXPENSE	PRICE	NOTES
PERMITTING & FEES		
PANELS		
PANEL STAND		
BATTERIES		
CHARGE CONTROLLERS		
INVERTER		
WIRING		
BREAKER		
GROUND RODS		
OUTLETS		
DISCONNECT		
CONTROL PANELS		
INSTALLATION		
INSULATION		
ADDITIONAL MATERIALS		
UNEXPECTED		
TOTAL:		

SEWAGE (SEPTIC SYSTEM, OUTHOUSE, COMPOSTING TOILET, INCINERATING TOILET, BIOGAS)

EXPENSE	PRICE	NOTES
PERMITTING & FEES		
CONTRACTOR FOR INSTALLATION		
IF NOT USING A CONTRACTOR		
TOOLS		
EXCAVATION		
SEPTIC TANKS		
PVC & DRAINAGE		
GRAVEL		
TOILET		
PIPING		
ADDITIONAL MATERIALS		
UNEXPECTED		
TOTAL:		

STORAGE

EXPENSE	PRICE	NOTES
PERMITTING & FEES		
ELECTRICAL & WIRING		
FOUNDATION		
STRUCTURE		
MATERIALS		
SHELVING		
UNEXPECTED		
TOTAL:		

GARDEN

EXPENSE	PRICE	NOTES
GREENHOUSE		
MATERIALS		
TOOLS		
TOTAL:		

SECURITY

EXPENSE	PRICE	NOTES
FENCING		
GATES		
CAMERAS		
LIGHTS		
LOCKS		
DOG		
FIREARMS		
TOTAL:		

ANIMALS

EXPENSE	PRICE	NOTES
BARN		
FENCING		
FEED BARRELS		
LIVESTOCK		
ADDITIONAL SUPPLIES		
TOTAL:		

OPTIONAL ITEMS

THIS IS WHERE YOU ADD ANY ADDITIONAL OUTBUILDINGS, LUXURY OR NEEDED ITEMS AND ANYTHING ELSE ON YOUR VISION BOARD.

EXPENSE	PRICE	NOTES
FARM VEHICLE		
TRACTOR		
PROPANE TANKS		
WIFI		
CELL SIGNAL BOOSTER		
TOTAL:		

NOTES

SUSTAINING OFFGRID LIVING: UNDERSTANDING THE CONTINUOUS NEED FOR INCOME

Transitioning to an offgrid lifestyle often conjures images of a self-sufficient utopia, free from the financial burdens of conventional living. However, the reality of offgrid life, while rich in freedom and simplicity, still carries the necessity for a continuous income stream. Ongoing expenses, often overlooked in the initial excitement of offgrid planning, play a critical role in maintaining and expanding your homestead.

Living off the grid does not exempt one from recurring costs such as insurance, which includes coverage for your farm, health, and vehicles. These are essential safeguards, protecting you against unexpected events and ensuring that your offgrid journey isn't derailed by unforeseen circumstances. Similarly, day-to-day necessities like toiletries, food staples that can't be grown or produced on-site, animal feed, and veterinary bills for livestock require a regular financial outlay.

Furthermore, an offgrid life is rarely static. Your homestead may evolve, necessitating investments in new infrastructure, tools, or technology. Whether it's expanding your solar array to meet increased energy needs, building additional structures, or investing in more efficient equipment, these growth initiatives require capital. Such expansions not only enhance the quality of your offgrid life but are often crucial for increasing the productivity and sustainability of your homestead.

Therefore, a key component of successful offgrid living is establishing reliable income streams. This could involve remote work, leveraging skills that are compatible with digital nomadism. For others, it may mean creating income-generating ventures on the homestead itself, such as selling produce, crafts, hosting workshops, or agritourism. The beauty of offgrid living is that it often provides the creative freedom to blend your lifestyle with income-producing activities that resonate with your values and skills.

It's also worth noting that the nature of these income streams may shift over time. As you settle into offgrid living, you might find new opportunities emerging from your specific environment or community. Keeping an open mind and being adaptable to these evolving opportunities is crucial.

While offgrid living can reduce many of the financial burdens of traditional lifestyles, it does not eliminate the need for a steady income. Planning for ongoing expenses and potential growth is essential in creating a sustainable, fulfilling, offgrid life. This for-ward-thinking approach ensures that your offgrid dream is supported by a realistic and viable financial strategy.

HOMESTEAD OPERATION WORKSHEET

Welcome to the Homestead Operation Worksheet, an essential tool designed to help you budget and plan for the ongoing operational costs of your offgrid homestead. This comprehensive worksheet will guide you through evaluating and estimating your regular expenses, ensuring you maintain a sustainable and financially stable offgrid lifestyle.

Instructions:

1. List of Expenses: Start by listing all potential ongoing expenses. This includes groceries, toiletries, insurance (health, farm, vehicle), internet, cell phone bills, animal feed, veterinary expenses, gardening supplies, existing debts (like car notes), homeschooling materials, and an emergency fund.

2. Monthly Expense Estimation: Next to each item, estimate your monthly expense. Be realistic in your estimations. It's better to overestimate than underestimate.

3. Debt and Loan Payments: Include any monthly debt or loan repayments, ensuring that these are prioritized in your budget.

5. Animal and Gardening Costs: Calculate the average monthly cost for animal feed and veterinary bills. For gardening, include expenses for seeds, tools, and other supplies.

6. Homeschooling Budget: If homeschooling is part of your plan, allocate a budget for educational materials and resources.

7. Emergency Fund: Decide on a monthly amount to set aside for unexpected expenses. This fund is crucial for handling unforeseen emergencies without disrupting your financial stability.

8. Total Monthly Budget: Sum up all the monthly expenses to calculate your total monthly budget. This gives you a clear idea of the regular financial commitment required to maintain your offgrid homestead.

9. Income vs. Expenses: Compare your total monthly budget with your expected monthly income. This will help you identify if there are any shortfalls and areas where you may need to cut back or find additional income.

10. Regular Review and Adjustment: It's important to regularly review this worksheet (at least quarterly) to adjust for changes in expenses or income. Offgrid living can be

dynamic, and your budget should be flexible enough to accommodate these changes.

By diligently filling out and regularly updating the Homestead Operation Worksheet, you'll be able to maintain a clear view of your financial health and ensure that your offgrid lifestyle remains sustainable and enjoyable. Remember, good financial planning is key to the success and longevity of your offgrid adventure.

GROCERIES		
TOILETRIES		
HOUSEHOLD SUPPLIES		
HEALTH INSURANCE		
PROPERTY INSURANCE		
VEHICLE INSURANCE		
INTERNET		
CELL PHONES		
ANIMAL FEED		
VET BILLS		
GARDENING & FARMING SUPPLIES		
FUEL COSTS (PROPANE, WOOD, ETC.)		
MAINTENANCE & REPAIRS		
DEBTS & LOAN PAYMENTS		
VEHICLE MAINTENANCE & FUEL		
HOMESCHOOL SUBSCRIPTIONS & SUPPLIES		
PROPERTY TAXES		
SAVINGS & INVESTMENTS		
ADDITIONAL		

NOTES

CRAFTING A REALISTIC TIMELINE FOR TRANSITIONING TO OFFGRID LIFE

Embarking on the journey to offgrid living is not only a shift in lifestyle but a complex project that demands careful planning and realistic timelines. The allure of a self-sufficient life, deeply connected with nature, is powerful, yet the path to achieving this dream is often paved with practical challenges and financial considerations. Crafting a realistic timeline for this transition is critical, taking into account your current financial situation, the capital needed for land purchase, building infrastructure, and other essentials.

First and foremost, a thorough evaluation of your finances is key. Understand your current financial health, including income, savings, debts, and how much you can realistically allocate toward your offgrid dream. This financial groundwork will help you determine the timeline for accumulating the necessary capital to purchase land and start building your offgrid infrastructure.

The nature of the infrastructure you plan to establish is directly proportional to your desired comfort level and, consequently, the budget and time required. For instance, a basic setup with minimal amenities will have different requirements and timelines compared to a more sophisticated, comfortable arrangement with advanced offgrid technologies. Your choice will influence not only the cost but also the complexity of the project.

When planning the build, factor in the complexity of each project, availability of resources, and most importantly, your skill level. If your plan includes structures or systems that require specialized skills, you might need to factor in time for learning these skills or budget for professional assistance. Also, resource availability, such as building materials, water sources, or renewable energy equipment, can greatly influence your timeline. In some cases, these resources may be readily available, while in others, they might need to be sourced from afar, adding to the time and cost.

Additionally, external factors such as weather conditions, permit processes, and local regulations can significantly impact your timeline. These aspects often lie outside your direct control and require a buffer in your planning.

Finally, it's important to maintain flexibility in your timeline. Offgrid projects can often encounter unforeseen challenges, and a rigid plan may lead to frustration. A well-thought-out, flexible timeline that accommodates potential delays and challenges will be a more practical and less stressful approach.

Transitioning to offgrid living is a significant undertaking that requires a realistic, well-structured timeline. This timeline should be grounded in a clear understanding of your financial capabilities, the scope and complexity of your offgrid projects, resource availability, skill set, and potential external factors. With careful planning and a flexible approach, the journey to offgrid living can be as fulfilling as the destination itself.

TRANSITION TIMELINE WORKSHEET

Instructions:

Use this worksheet to help determine a realistic timeframe for your transition to an off-grid lifestyle. Consider the different aspects and milestones involved in the process. Assess each section and estimate the time required for completion. Remember that timelines may vary depending on individual circumstances and goals.

Determine the amount of time needed for research on offgrid living, including climate, regulations, infrastructure, and lifestyle considerations.

_____

_____

_____

Allocate time for creating a comprehensive offgrid plan, including identifying land, assessing financial resources, and developing a budget.

_____

_____

_____

Estimate the time required for finding suitable land that meets your offgrid requirements.

_____

_____

_____

Account for visiting potential properties, conducting inspections, negotiating, and finalizing the purchase.

_____

_____

Assess the time needed for developing essential offgrid infrastructure, such as building or renovating structures, installing renewable energy systems, and establishing water and waste management systems.

_____

_____

_____

Consider the complexity of the projects, availability of resources, and your skill level or the need for professional assistance.

_____

_____

_____

Allocate time for acquiring new skills necessary for offgrid living, such as gardening, animal husbandry, renewable energy system maintenance, and basic construction.

_____

_____

_____

Research training options, workshops, or online courses that can help you gain the required knowledge and expertise.

_____

_____

_____

Estimate the time needed to save or acquire the necessary funds for purchasing land, developing infrastructure, and covering ongoing expenses.

_____

_____

Consider your current financial situation, income sources, and potential adjustments to optimize savings.

_____

_____

_____

Determine the time required for the actual transition to offgrid living.

_____

_____

_____

Schedule periodic reviews to assess your progress, make adjustments to your timeline if necessary, and celebrate milestones achieved.

Note: This worksheet is intended to provide a general framework for planning your off-grid transition timeline. Adapt the timeline to your specific circumstances, resources, and goals. Remember that flexibility and adaptability are key during the offgrid journey.

NOTES

LOCATING YOUR OFFGRID HOMESTEAD: BEYOND GEOGRAPHY TO A SYMPHONY OF FACTORS

Finding the perfect spot for your offgrid homestead goes beyond just the allure of scenic vistas or remote tranquility. It's a decision interwoven with a myriad of considerations, each playing a pivotal role in shaping the success and sustainability of your offgrid journey. From the practical to the political, each factor must be weighed and balanced, underscoring the immense importance of thorough research in this initial phase.

First and foremost, climate plays a central role. It determines not just the kind of crops you can grow, but also the type of dwellings appropriate for the region, the efficiency of solar or wind energy, and even the availability of water. A location with prolonged winters might require more robust heating solutions, while arid regions will necessitate efficient water harvesting and storage systems.

Terrain, too, is crucial. The lay of the land influences everything from construction feasibility to water runoff and soil fertility. A hilly landscape might offer breathtaking views but could present challenges in building or farming. Conversely, flatlands might ease construction but may require added considerations for drainage.

Beyond the natural elements, the political climate of a region is equally consequential. Local regulations, building codes, and land use policies can significantly impact the feasibility of certain offgrid setups. Some regions might be supportive of alternative housing structures, like yurts or earthships, while others may have strict guidelines that could curtail such aspirations.

Weather patterns, while seemingly a subset of climate, deserve special attention. Being aware of seasonal fluctuations, the likelihood of extreme weather events, or even the changing patterns due to global climate shifts can be instrumental in long-term planning.

However, all these factors, vital as they are, underscore one overarching truth: the decision about where to set up your offgrid homestead cannot be taken lightly or hastily. It demands rigorous research, site visits, and often, consultations with local experts and existing offgridders. This process, while intensive, ensures that when you finally settle on a location, it aligns not just with your dreams but with the intricate tapestry of elements that will determine your offgrid success.

LOCATION FINDING WORKSHEET

Welcome to the Location Finding Worksheet, a vital tool in YOUR Offgrid planning journey. This worksheet is designed to assist you in determining a general location for your offgrid homestead, especially if you haven't already settled on a specific area. By evaluating various environmental, geographical, and socio-political factors, this worksheet will help you narrow down your choices to a specific county or region that best suits your offgrid living goals.

Instructions:

1. List Potential Locations: Start by listing potential states, regions, or countries you are considering. These should be places you're initially drawn to based on your basic preferences or research.

2. Climate Preferences: Under each location, note down your climate preferences, such as temperature range, humidity levels, and seasonal variations. This will help you identify areas that match your comfort and lifestyle needs.

3. Severe Weather Evaluation: Research and record the frequency and types of severe weather events (like hurricanes, tornadoes, wildfires) each area experiences. Consider how comfortable you are with these risks.

4. Sunshine and Rainfall Analysis: Document the average amount of yearly sunshine and annual rainfall for each location. This information is crucial for planning your solar energy solutions and water harvesting systems.

5. Topographical Considerations: Note the topographical features of each area (mountainous, flatlands, forested, etc.) and how they align with your vision for offgrid living (like farming needs, building constraints, etc.).

6. Political Climate: Investigate and jot down notes on the political climate of each region, especially focusing on land use laws, building codes, and offgrid living regulations.

This worksheet is a dynamic tool in your offgrid planning process. Your preferences and requirements might evolve as you delve deeper into planning, so feel free to revisit and adjust your Location Finding Worksheet as needed. The goal is to find a location that not only meets your practical needs but also resonates with your aspirations for offgrid living.

LOCATION FINDING WORKSHEET 1

Climate _____

_____

Region _____

_____

State _____

_____

Counties_____

_____

Politics _____

_____

Severe weather _____

_____

Amount of yearly sunshine for solar _____

_____

Annual rainfall _____

_____

Additional Notes

LOCATION FINDING WORKSHEET 2

Climate _____

_____

Region _____

_____

State _____

_____

Counties_____

_____

Politics _____

_____

Severe weather _____

_____

Amount of yearly sunshine for solar _____

_____

Annual rainfall _____

_____

Additional Notes

LOCATION FINDING WORKSHEET 3

Climate _____

_____

Region _____

_____

State _____

_____

Counties_____

_____

Politics _____

_____

Severe weather _____

_____

Amount of yearly sunshine for solar _____

_____

Annual rainfall _____

_____

Additional Notes

LOCATION FINDING WORKSHEET 4

Climate _____

_____

Region _____

_____

State _____

_____

Counties_____

_____

Politics _____

_____

Severe weather _____

_____

Amount of yearly sunshine for solar _____

_____

Annual rainfall _____

_____

Additional Notes

NOTES

NAVIGATING THE TAPESTRY OF REGULATIONS: THE IMPERATIVE OF LOCAL DUE DILIGENCE

The allure of offgrid living often carries with it images of boundless freedom, a life unshackled from societal constraints, and an immersion into nature's embrace. However, beneath this vision lies a more intricate reality governed by a web of rules, regulations, and local ordinances. This makes the seemingly simple act of purchasing land for an offgrid lifestyle a task that demands meticulous research, especially at the city or county level.

Before investing in a parcel of land, reaching out to local authorities is not just a formality—it's an essential step that can mean the difference between the realization of your offgrid dream and unforeseen roadblocks. Local governments often have zoning regulations, building codes, and land use policies that can significantly impact, or even prohibit, certain offgrid endeavors.

For instance, while a piece of land may seem perfect for your envisioned home, local building codes might strictly dictate the types of permissible structures, rendering your plans unviable. Similarly, regulations concerning septic systems, water collection, and even the installation of solar panels can vary widely from one jurisdiction to another. In some places, there might even be mandates requiring homes to be connected to the municipal power grid or water supply.

Why do these regulations exist? They're often rooted in concerns about safety, environmental preservation, or community standards. And while they might sometimes feel restrictive, they may possibly serve a purpose in ensuring the well-being of residents and the land.

By proactively contacting city or county offices, potential offgridders can gain a clear understanding of what's allowed, what's restricted, and what might require special permissions. This knowledge not only prevents potential legal disputes and financial losses but also allows for informed decisions, ensuring that the chosen land truly aligns with one's offgrid aspirations.

In essence, while the spirit of offgrid living is anchored in autonomy and self-reliance, it must coexist with the rules of the land in the most literal sense. Thorough due diligence at the local level is a cornerstone of this harmonious coexistence, ensuring that the journey to offgrid living begins on solid, informed ground.

WHAT TO ASK THE COUNTY/CITY 1

Use this worksheet to help you evaluate whether a specific area is suitable for your offgrid living goals by examining various regulations and requirements.

Instructions:

1. Contact Local Authorities: Reach out to the local Planning and Zoning Department or relevant authorities to gather information on the following topics. It's crucial to review all applicable codes and regulations for your desired area.

2. Rate Each Category: After gathering information, rate each category on a scale of 1 to 5, with 1 being highly restrictive and 5 being very friendly to offgrid living.

3. Ask Questions: Don't hesitate to ask questions to clarify any doubts or uncertainties regard-ing the regulations. You do not have to provide any of your personal information.

4. Verification: Make sure to ask where you can find all of the written codes and regula-tions. Do not just trust the word of the person on the other side of the phone without verifying all information.

Location/Area Name: _____

County: _____

City/Town: _____

Contact Information for Local Planning and Zoning Department: _____

_____

1. Power Grid Connection:

• Is it possible to disconnect from the power grid?

_____

_____

_____

• Are there any restrictions on using solar or wind energy systems?

_____

_____

_____

Rating: _____ (1-5)

2. Water Sources:

• Are there regulations regarding well drilling?

_____

_____

_____

• Are there restrictions on collecting rainwater?

_____

_____

_____

• Are there water usage restrictions?

_____

_____

_____

Rating: _____ (1-5)

3. Waste Management:

• What are there regulations and requirements for managing waste?

_____

_____

_____

• Is a septic system required? If so, are there any specific regulations like a PERC test, distance from other structures, does it have to be professionally installed?

_____

_____

_____

• Is a composting toilet or alternative waste management allowed?

_____

_____

_____

• Do you still need a septic system for graywater even if you have a composting toilet, incinerating toilet, or outhouse?

_____

_____

_____

Rating: _____ (1-5)

4. Housing Restrictions:

• Are there restrictions on the type of housing, such as RVs, tiny homes, mobile homes, or minimum square footage?

_____

_____

_____

• What are the building requirements, including permits and inspections?

_____

_____

_____

Rating: _____ (1-5)

5. Animal and Livestock Regulations:

• Is there a minimum acreage required for keeping animals or livestock?

_____

_____

_____

• Are there specific restrictions on the types or numbers of animals allowed?

_____

_____

_____

Rating: _____ (1-5)

6. Additional Information:

• Are there any hunting or fishing restrictions?

_____

_____

_____

• Is there anything else that I may need to know?

_____

_____

_____

Overall Evaluation:

• Based on the ratings, do you consider this area to be offgrid friendly? (Yes/No)

• If yes, what aspects make it favorable for offgrid living?

_____

_____

_____

• If no, what are the major obstacles or restrictions?

_____

_____

_____

Additional Notes: Remember that this worksheet serves as a preliminary evaluation tool. Review all applicable codes and consult with local authorities and experts to gain a comprehensive understanding of the area's regulations before making any decisions about your offgrid living plans.

WHAT TO ASK THE COUNTY/CITY 2

Use this worksheet to help you evaluate whether a specific area is suitable for your offgrid living goals by examining various regulations and requirements.

Instructions:

1. Contact Local Authorities: Reach out to the local Planning and Zoning Department or relevant authorities to gather information on the following topics. It's crucial to review all applicable codes and regulations for your desired area.

2. Rate Each Category: After gathering information, rate each category on a scale of 1 to 5, with 1 being highly restrictive and 5 being very friendly to offgrid living.

3. Ask Questions: Don't hesitate to ask questions to clarify any doubts or uncertainties regard-ing the regulations. You do not have to provide any of your personal information.

4. Verification: Make sure to ask where you can find all of the written codes and regula-tions. Do not just trust the word of the person on the other side of the phone without verifying all information.

Location/Area Name: _____

County: _____

City/Town: _____

Contact Information for Local Planning and Zoning Department: _____

_____

1. Power Grid Connection:

• Is it possible to disconnect from the power grid?

_____

_____

• Are there any restrictions on using solar or wind energy systems?

_____

_____

_____

Rating: _____ (1-5)

2. Water Sources:

• Are there regulations regarding well drilling?

_____

_____

_____

• Are there restrictions on collecting rainwater?

_____

_____

_____

• Are there water usage restrictions?

_____

_____

_____

Rating: _____ (1-5)

3. Waste Management:

• What are there regulations and requirements for managing waste?

_____

_____

_____

• Is a septic system required? If so, are there any specific regulations like a PERC test, distance from other structures, does it have to be professionally installed?

_____

_____

_____

• Is a composting toilet or alternative waste management allowed?

_____

_____

_____

• Do you still need a septic system for graywater even if you have a composting toilet, incinerating toilet, or outhouse?

_____

_____

_____

Rating: _____ (1-5)

4. Housing Restrictions:

• Are there restrictions on the type of housing, such as RVs, tiny homes, mobile homes, or minimum square footage?

_____

_____

_____

• What are the building requirements, including permits and inspections?

_____

_____

_____

Rating: _____ (1-5)

5. Animal and Livestock Regulations:

• Is there a minimum acreage required for keeping animals or livestock?

_____

_____

_____

• Are there specific restrictions on the types or numbers of animals allowed?

_____

_____

_____

Rating: _____ (1-5)

6. Additional Information:

• Are there any hunting or fishing restrictions?

_____

_____

• Is there anything else that I may need to know?

_____

_____

_____

Overall Evaluation:

• Based on the ratings, do you consider this area to be offgrid friendly? (Yes/No)

• If yes, what aspects make it favorable for offgrid living?

_____

_____

_____

• If no, what are the major obstacles or restrictions?

_____

_____

_____

Additional Notes: Remember that this worksheet serves as a preliminary evaluation tool. Review all applicable codes and consult with local authorities and experts to gain a comprehensive understanding of the area's regulations before making any decisions about your offgrid living plans.

WHAT TO ASK THE COUNTY/CITY 3

Use this worksheet to help you evaluate whether a specific area is suitable for your offgrid living goals by examining various regulations and requirements.

Instructions:

1. Contact Local Authorities: Reach out to the local Planning and Zoning Department or relevant authorities to gather information on the following topics. It's crucial to review all applicable codes and regulations for your desired area.

2. Rate Each Category: After gathering information, rate each category on a scale of 1 to 5, with 1 being highly restrictive and 5 being very friendly to offgrid living.

3. Ask Questions: Don't hesitate to ask questions to clarify any doubts or uncertainties regard-ing the regulations. You do not have to provide any of your personal information.

4. Verification: Make sure to ask where you can find the all of the written codes and regu-lations. Do not just trust the word of the person on the other side of the phone without verifying all information.

Location/Area Name: _____

County: _____

City/Town: _____

Contact Information for Local Planning and Zoning Department: _____

_____

1. Power Grid Connection:

• Is it possible to disconnect from the power grid?

_____

_____

_____

• Are there any restrictions on using solar or wind energy systems?

_____

_____

_____

Rating: _____ (1-5)

2. Water Sources:

• Are there regulations regarding well drilling?

_____

_____

_____

• Are there restrictions on collecting rainwater?

_____

_____

_____

• Are there water usage restrictions?

_____

_____

_____

Rating: _____ (1-5)

3. Waste Management:

• What are there regulations and requirements for managing waste?

_____

_____

_____

• Is a septic system required? If so, are there any specific regulations like a PERC test, distance from other structures, does it have to be professionally installed?

_____

_____

_____

• Is a composting toilet or alternative waste management allowed?

_____

_____

_____

• Do you still need a septic system for graywater even if you have a composting toilet, incinerating toilet, or outhouse?

_____

_____

_____

Rating: _____ (1-5)

4. Housing Restrictions:

• Are there restrictions on the type of housing, such as RVs, tiny homes, mobile homes, or minimum square footage?

_____

_____

_____

• What are the building requirements, including permits and inspections?

_____

_____

_____

Rating: _____ (1-5)

5. Animal and Livestock Regulations:

• Is there a minimum acreage required for keeping animals or livestock?

_____

_____

_____

• Are there specific restrictions on the types or numbers of animals allowed?

_____

_____

_____

Rating: _____ (1-5)

6. Additional Information:

• Are there any hunting or fishing restrictions?

_____

_____

_____

• Is there anything else that I may need to know?

_____

_____

Overall Evaluation:

• Based on the ratings, do you consider this area to be offgrid friendly? (Yes/No)

• If yes, what aspects make it favorable for offgrid living?

_____

_____

_____

• If no, what are the major obstacles or restrictions?

_____

_____

_____

Additional Notes: Remember that this worksheet serves as a preliminary evaluation tool. Review all applicable codes and consult with local authorities and experts to gain a comprehensive understanding of the area's regulations before making any decisions about your offgrid living plans.

WHAT TO ASK THE COUNTY/CITY 4

Use this worksheet to help you evaluate whether a specific area is suitable for your offgrid living goals by examining various regulations and requirements.

Instructions:

1. Contact Local Authorities: Reach out to the local Planning and Zoning Department or relevant authorities to gather information on the following topics. It's crucial to review all applicable codes and regulations for your desired area.

2. Rate Each Category: After gathering information, rate each category on a scale of 1 to 5, with 1 being highly restrictive and 5 being very friendly to offgrid living.

3. Ask Questions: Don't hesitate to ask questions to clarify any doubts or uncertainties regard-ing the regulations. You do not have to provide any of your personal information.

4. Verification: Make sure to ask where you can find all of the written codes and regulations. Do not just trust the word of the person on the other side of the phone without verifying all information.

Location/Area Name: _____

County: _____

City/Town: _____

Contact Information for Local Planning and Zoning Department: _____

_____

1. Power Grid Connection:

• Is it possible to disconnect from the power grid?

_____

_____

• Are there any restrictions on using solar or wind energy systems?

_____

_____

_____

Rating: _____ (1-5)

2. Water Sources:

• Are there regulations regarding well drilling?

_____

_____

_____

• Are there restrictions on collecting rainwater?

_____

_____

_____

• Are there water usage restrictions?

_____

_____

_____

Rating: _____ (1-5)

3. Waste Management:

• What are there regulations and requirements for managing waste?

_____

_____

_____

• Is a septic system required? If so, are there any specific regulations like a PERC test, distance from other structures, does it have to be professionally installed?

_____

_____

_____

• Is a composting toilet or alternative waste management allowed?

_____

_____

_____

• Do you still need a septic system for graywater even if you have a composting toilet, incinerating toilet, or outhouse?

_____

_____

_____

Rating: _____ (1-5)

4. Housing Restrictions:

• Are there restrictions on the type of housing, such as RVs, tiny homes, mobile homes, or minimum square footage?

_____

_____

_____

• What are the building requirements, including permits and inspections?

_____

_____

_____

Rating: _____ (1-5)

5. Animal and Livestock Regulations:

• Is there a minimum acreage required for keeping animals or livestock?

_____

_____

_____

• Are there specific restrictions on the types or numbers of animals allowed?

_____

_____

_____

Rating: _____ (1-5)

6. Additional Information:

• Are there any hunting or fishing restrictions?

_____

_____

• Is there anything else that I may need to know?

_____

_____

_____

Overall Evaluation:

• Based on the ratings, do you consider this area to be offgrid friendly? (Yes/No)

• If yes, what aspects make it favorable for offgrid living?

_____

_____

_____

• If no, what are the major obstacles or restrictions?

_____

_____

_____

Additional Notes: Remember that this worksheet serves as a preliminary evaluation tool. Review all applicable codes and consult with local authorities and experts to gain a comprehensive understanding of the area's regulations before making any decisions about your offgrid living plans.

NOTES

_____

_____

_____

_____

_____

_____

_____

_____

_____

_____

_____

_____

_____

_____

_____

_____

_____

_____

_____

_____

NAVIGATING THE LAND BUYING PROCESS FOR YOUR OFFGRID HOMESTEAD

The process of buying land for your offgrid homestead is a pivotal step in your journey towards self-sufficiency and a deeper connection with nature. It's a process that requires careful consideration and thorough research.

First and foremost, you must define your criteria for the ideal piece of land. Consider factors such as location, climate, terrain, and proximity to essential resources like water and potential neighbors. This initial vision will serve as your compass as you navigate the real estate market.

Next, you'll need to secure financing or set a budget. Land prices can vary significantly based on location, size, and available amenities. Having a clear understanding of your financial boundaries will help narrow down your options and prevent you from overextending.

Once you've established your budget, it's time to start searching for available properties. Utilize online listings, real estate agents, and local resources to identify potential parcels of land. Visit the sites in person to get a firsthand feel for the land, its surroundings, and whether it aligns with your vision.

When you've identified a property that meets your criteria, it's crucial to conduct due diligence. This involves researching the property's history, boundaries, zoning regulations, and any potential restrictions that may affect your offgrid plans. You may also want to have the land surveyed to ensure accurate boundaries.

The negotiation and purchase phase follows, during which you'll make an offer, negotiate terms, and secure financing if necessary. Working with a real estate attorney or agent can be highly beneficial during this stage to ensure a smooth transaction and protect your interests.

Finally, once the deal is finalized, you'll acquire the land title and begin the process of turning your newfound property into your offgrid haven. It's a journey that requires patience, research, and careful decision-making, but with the right approach, you'll soon have the foundation for your offgrid dream.

PROPERTY BUYING WORKSHEET INSTRUCTIONS

The Property Buying Worksheet is a key component of your "Offgrid Planning Workbook," designed to assist you in evaluating potential properties for your offgrid homestead. This tool is essential for conducting thorough due diligence, ensuring that each property you consider aligns with your specific goals and dreams. By methodically analyzing each property before visiting, you can save time and resources, focusing only on those options that truly meet your criteria.

Instructions:

1. Property Details: - Begin by listing the basic details of each property you are considering, including location, size, price, and listing agent contact information.

2. Land Characteristics & Topography: Evaluate the land's characteristics, such as soil quality, existing vegetation, water sources, topography, and access to roads. Consider how these features align with your offgrid needs (like agriculture, building sites, etc.).

3. Resource Availability: Document the availability and accessibility of essential resources, including water (wells, streams, rainwater potential), wood (for building or heating), and sun exposure (for solar energy).

4. Infrastructure and Utilities: Note any existing infrastructure, such as buildings, fences, or roads, and the status of utilities like electricity, sewage, and internet connectivity.

5. Environmental Risks: Assess environmental risks associated with each property, including flood zones, wildfire risk, and exposure to natural disasters.

6. Community and Surrounding: Consider the surrounding community, neighborhood, and proximity to essential services like markets, hospitals, and schools.

7. Legal Considerations: Investigate any legal considerations, including property taxes, easements, and rights of way.

8. Long-term Potential: Evaluate the long-term potential of the property, including expansion possibilities, resale value, and any future developments planned in the area.

9. Personal Impression and Fit: Note your personal impressions of each property from the

listing and any additional research. Does it feel like the right fit for your offgrid vision?

10. Prioritization and Shortlisting: Rank the properties based on how well they align with your criteria. Shortlist those that most closely meet your needs.

12. Visitation Planning: Plan visits to the top-ranked properties to get a firsthand impression and gather more detailed information.

13. Final Evaluation: After visiting, revisit the worksheet to update your impressions and information. This final evaluation will help you make a well-informed decision.

Remember, the Property Buying Worksheet is not just a checklist; it's a framework to guide your critical thinking and ensure that you're making informed decisions. Each property you consider should be thoroughly vetted through this lens to ensure it aligns with your offgrid aspirations and practical requirements.

PROPERTY BUYING WORKSHEET 1

Use this checklist to compare properties

Address _____

County _____

Price _____

Financing available _____

Lot Size _____

Topography _____

Infrastructure available _____

Water Sources _____

Buildings on property _____

Fencing _____

Roads _____

Zoning _____

Flood zone? _____

Average well depths (Call local well driller) _____

_____

Access & easements _____

_____

Cell signal _____

Land survey _____

_____

Water rights _____

_____

Mineral rights _____

_____

Timber rights _____

Crime in the area?_____

_____

Distance from shopping _____

_____

Distance from hospital _____

_____

School ratings _____

_____

Neighbors & Community _____

_____

Soil quality _____

_____

Property taxes _____

_____

Covenants & HOA fees _____

_____

Title Insurance is a must! _____

Is the size big enough to accommodate future growth? _____

_____

Does vegetation/trees need to be cleared? _____

Are roads accessible year-round? _____

Impression: _____

Does it fit your current goals & future growth? _____

_____

NOTES

PROPERTY BUYING WORKSHEET 2

Use this checklist to compare properties

Address _____

County _____

Price _____

Financing available _____

Lot Size _____

Topography _____

Infrastructure available _____

Water Sources _____

Buildings on property _____

Fencing _____

Roads _____

Zoning _____

Flood zone? _____

Average well depths (Call local well driller) _____

_____

Access & easements _____

_____

Cell signal _____

Land survey _____

_____

Water rights _____

_____

Mineral rights _____

_____

Timber rights _____

Crime in the area? _____

_____

Distance from shopping _____

_____

Distance from hospital _____

_____

School ratings _____

_____

Neighbors & Community _____

_____

Soil quality _____

_____

Property taxes _____

_____

Covenants & HOA fees _____

_____

_____

Title Insurance is a must! _____

Is the size big enough to accommodate future growth? _____

_____

Does vegetation/trees need to be cleared? _____

Are roads accessible year-round? _____

Impression: _____

Does it fit your current goals & future growth? _____

_____

NOTES

PROPERTY BUYING WORKSHEET 3

Use this checklist to compare properties

Address _____

County _____

Price _____

Financing available _____

Lot Size _____

Topography _____

Infrastructure available _____

Water Sources _____

Buildings on property _____

Fencing _____

Roads _____

Zoning _____

Flood zone? _____

Average well depths (Call local well driller) _____

_____

Access & easements _____

_____

Cell signal _____

Land survey _____

_____

Water rights _____

_____

Mineral rights _____

_____

Timber rights _____

Crime in the area? _____

_____

Distance from shopping _____

_____

Distance from hospital _____

_____

School ratings _____

_____

Neighbors & Community _____

_____

Soil quality _____

_____

Property taxes _____

_____

Covenants & HOA fees _____

_____

Title Insurance is a must! _____

Is the size big enough to accommodate future growth? _____

_____

Does vegetation/trees need to be cleared? _____

Are roads accessible year-round? _____

Impression: _____

Does it fit your current goals & future growth? _____

_____

NOTES

PROPERTY BUYING WORKSHEET 4

Use this checklist to compare properties

Address _____

County _____

Price _____

Financing available _____

Lot Size _____

Topography _____

Infrastructure available _____

Water Sources _____

Buildings on property _____

Fencing _____

Roads _____

Zoning _____

Flood zone? _____

Average well depths (Call local well driller) _____

_____

Access & easements _____

_____

Cell signal _____

Land survey _____

_____

Water rights _____

_____

Mineral rights _____

_____

Timber rights _____

Crime in the area? _____

_____

Distance from shopping _____

_____

Distance from hospital _____

_____

School ratings _____

_____

Neighbors & Community _____

_____

Soil quality _____

_____

Property taxes _____

_____

Covenants & HOA fees _____

_____

Title Insurance is a must! _____

Is the size big enough to accommodate future growth? _____

_____

Does vegetation/trees need to be cleared? _____

Are roads accessible year-round? _____

Impression: _____

Does it fit your current goals & future growth? _____

_____

NOTES

OFFGRID
HOMESTEAD
FAM

Planned Visit Date  _____

PROPERTY BUYING WORKSHEET 5

Use this checklist to compare properties

Address _____

County _____

Price _____

Financing available _____

Lot Size _____

Topography _____

Infrastructure available _____

Water Sources _____

Buildings on property _____

Fencing _____

Roads _____

Zoning _____

Flood zone? _____

Average well depths (Call local well driller) _____

_____

Access & easements _____

_____

Cell signal _____

Land survey _____

_____

Water rights _____

_____

Mineral rights _____

_____

Timber rights _____

Crime in the area? _____

_____

Distance from shopping _____

_____

Distance from hospital _____

_____

School ratings _____

_____

Neighbors & Community _____

_____

Soil quality _____

_____

Property taxes _____

_____

Covenants & HOA fees _____

_____

Title Insurance is a must! _____

Is the size big enough to accommodate future growth? _____

_____

Does vegetation/trees need to be cleared? _____

Are roads accessible year-round? _____

Impression: _____

Does it fit your current goals & future growth? _____

_____

NOTES

Planned Visit Date _____

PROPERTY BUYING WORKSHEET 6

Use this checklist to compare properties

Address _____

County _____

Price _____

Financing available _____

Lot Size _____

Topography _____

Infrastructure available _____

Water Sources _____

Buildings on property _____

Fencing _____

Roads _____

Zoning _____

Flood zone? _____

Average well depths (Call local well driller) _____

_____

Access & easements _____

_____

Cell signal _____

Land survey _____

_____

Water rights _____

_____

Mineral rights _____

_____

Timber rights _____

Crime in the area? _____

_____

Distance from shopping _____

_____

Distance from hospital _____

_____

School ratings _____

_____

Neighbors & Community _____

_____

Soil quality _____

_____

Property taxes _____

_____

Covenants & HOA fees _____

_____

Title Insurance is a must! _____

Is the size big enough to accommodate future growth? _____

_____

Does vegetation/trees need to be cleared? _____

Are roads accessible year-round? _____

Impression: _____

Does it fit your current goals & future growth? _____

_____

NOTES

STRATEGIC SEQUENCING IN OFFGRID HOMESTEAD SETUP: EMBRACING PATIENCE AND REALISM

When venturing into the realm of offgrid living, the excitement of building a self-sufficient lifestyle is palpable. However, without careful prioritization and strategic sequencing of your homestead setup and subsequent projects, this dream can swiftly become an overwhelming and daunting endeavor. The importance of meticulously planning the sequence of tasks cannot be overstated, as it is crucial for a smooth and successful transition to offgrid living.

The very nature of establishing an offgrid homestead involves a complex interplay of various projects—from constructing dwellings and setting up renewable energy sources to establishing water systems and growing food. Each of these tasks demands a unique blend of time, finances, and resources. Prioritizing these tasks in a logical and practical sequence is essential.

Start by identifying the foundational elements needed for basic functioning and safety. This often includes securing a reliable water source, shelter, and a basic energy setup. These are non-negotiables that provide the framework for more elaborate projects down the line. For instance, without a stable water source, efforts towards establishing a garden or maintaining livestock may be futile.

Next, consider the financial aspects. Certain projects may have upfront costs that are higher but are essential for reducing long-term expenses. For example, investing in a robust solar power system might be costly initially but can significantly reduce energy costs in the long run. Aligning project execution with your financial capacity ensures that you do not overextend your resources at any given point.

Furthermore, the sequencing of projects should reflect the availability and allocation of resources, including human resources. Some tasks may require specific skills or additional labor. Timing these projects when you have access to these resources can make the process more efficient and less stressful.

Additionally, it's important to factor in the temporal aspects—some projects may be seasonally dependent. Planting seasons, weather patterns, and daylight hours will dictate the feasibility and timing of certain tasks.

Without proper prioritization, there's a risk of misallocating resources, running out of funds, or becoming bogged down with too many simultaneous projects. This can not only stall your progress but also lead to a sense of frustration and burnout.

It's crucial to remember that building a homestead takes time. Having realistic expectations about the timeline for completing all the additional projects after the initial infrastructure is essential. For many, creating the complete homestead of their dreams is a journey that unfolds over years. It's important to relish the process, celebrating each small victory along the way. Embracing patience and enjoying the gradual evolution of your homestead will not only make the journey more enjoyable but also more rewarding in the long term.

The key to a successful and enjoyable offgrid transition lies in the art of prioritizing and sequencing your homestead setup tasks. By taking into account the interdependencies of time, finance, and resources, and by tackling projects in a logical order, you can ensure that your offgrid adventure unfolds in a manageable, fulfilling, and sustainable way, all while savoring the journey itself.

OFFGRID PROJECT PRIORITIZATION WORKSHEET

Purpose:

The Offgrid Project Prioritization Worksheet is designed to help you systematically organize and prioritize the various projects and infrastructure developments necessary for your offgrid transition. This tool emphasizes the importance of aligning these projects with your personal comfort preferences, ensuring that your offgrid lifestyle not only becomes sustainable but also enjoyable and aligned with your expectations.

Instructions:

1. List All Projects: Begin by listing every project you anticipate needing for your offgrid setup. This can include land clearing, building a main house, setting up solar panels, establishing a water system, creating a garden, and more.

2. Define Comfort Preferences: Next to each project, note down how it aligns with your personal comfort preferences. For example, if a reliable internet connection is crucial for your comfort, prioritize projects related to communication infrastructure.

3. Evaluate Necessity and Impact: For each project, assess its necessity and impact on your overall offgrid living. How essential is it for basic functioning, and how much does it contributes to your desired quality of life?

4. Estimate Cost and Complexity: Provide an estimate of the cost and complexity for each project. This will help you understand the resources needed and the scale of the effort involved.

5. Timeline Considerations: Note any time-sensitive projects or those that need to be completed by a certain season (like planting a garden).

6. Skill and Resource Assessment: Assess the skills and resources required for each project. Identify which projects you can do yourself and which might require professional help.

7. Prioritization Ranking: Using the information above, rank each project in order of priority. Consider both the necessity for basic living and your personal comfort preferences.

8. Phase Planning: Divide your projects into phases based on priority, cost, and timeline.

For instance, Phase 1 could include all high-priority projects necessary for initial living, while Phase 2 could focus on projects that enhance comfort and lifestyle.

9. Contingency Planning: Have a contingency plan for unexpected delays or challenges. Be prepared to adjust your priorities as needed.

10. Review and Adjustment: Regularly review and adjust your prioritization as your offgrid transition progresses. Be flexible in adapting to new information or changes in your situation.

Note: Remember, prioritizing offgrid projects is a balance between practical necessities and personal preferences. Your comfort and satisfaction are key to a successful and sustainable offgrid lifestyle.

PROJECT	COST	TIME TO COMPLETE	NOTES
HOUSING			
WATER			
SEWAGE			
ELECTRICITY			

USED RV CHECKLIST INSTRUCTIONS

Purchasing a used RV can be an exciting step towards freedom and adventure. However, it's crucial to thoroughly inspect any potential purchase to ensure it meets your needs and doesn't harbor hidden problems. The Used RV Checklist is designed to guide you through a comprehensive inspection process, helping you make an informed decision and avoid costly mistakes.

Instructions:

1. Pre-Inspection Preparation: Before you go to see the RV, equip yourself with necessary tools like a flashlight, measuring tape, notepad, and a camera or smartphone for taking pictures.

2. Exterior Inspection:

   - Check the RV's body for any signs of damage, such as dents, rust, or cracks. Pay special attention to the roof, undercarriage, and sidewalls.

   - Inspect the tires for wear and tear, check the tread depth, and look for any cracks or bulges.

3. Structural Integrity: Examine the frame for any signs of damage or repairs. Look out for any warping or rust that could indicate structural issues.

4. Interior Inspection:

   - Inside the RV, check for any signs of leaks, water damage, or mold, especially around windows, doors, and the roof.

   - Test all doors, drawers, and cabinets for smooth operation and stability.

5. Appliances and Systems:

   - Test all appliances, including the refrigerator, stove, oven, microwave, and air conditioning, to ensure they are fully functional.

   - Check the plumbing system by running faucets, flushing the toilet, and looking for leaks or water damage.

6. Electrical Systems:

- Test all electrical components, including lights, outlets, and any electronic gadgets.

- If possible, inspect the wiring for any frayed wires or loose connections.

7. Engine and Mechanics:

   - If it's a motorhome, inspect the engine, brakes, and transmission. Look for any leaks or unusual noises.

   - Check the vehicle's service history and ask about the frequency and type of maintenance it has received.

8. Safety Features: Ensure that safety features like smoke detectors, carbon monoxide detectors, and fire extinguishers are present and functional.

9. Comfort and Convenience:

   - Consider the RV's layout and whether it meets your needs in terms of space, storage, and comfort.

   - Check for additional features like an awning, satellite dish, or extra storage compartments.

10. Documentation Check:

   - Ask to see all relevant documents, including the title, registration, and any maintenance records.

11. Final Assessment:

   - After the inspection, take some time to assess whether the RV fits your needs and budget.

   - Consider any repair or upgrade costs identified during the inspection.

Remember, taking your time and being thorough during the inspection can save you from future headaches. Use the checklist as a guide, but also trust your instincts. If something feels off, it's worth investigating further or considering other options.

USED RV INSPECTION CHECKLIST

What to bring: a generator, flashlight, tire pressure gauge, toolbox (complete with screwdrivers and pliers), gloves, multimeter, electric outlet tester, usb outlet tester

• Make/Model	
• Year	
• Mileage	
• Asking Price	
• Width	
• Height	
• Weight	
• Tank Capacities — Fuel, propane, freshwater, graywater, and black water	
PLUMBING	
Examine the entire RV for leaks by filling the freshwater tank and turning on faucets.	
Ensure that the toilet flushes, the drains empty quickly and that gauges are accurate.	
PROPANE	
Make sure there are no leaks when turning the gas on, then check all appliances that operate with propane.	

USED RV INSPECTION CHECKLIST

GENERATOR	Start the generator to hear how loud it is, give it a visual inspection, and make sure the specs are sufficient for your use.
Operation	
Overall condition	
Gas capacity	
Fluid levels	
INTERIOR	
Windows and doors: Look for cracks or discoloration and examine all the seals on the interior as well.	
Make sure all windows and doors open and close without issue. (RV windows are a critical fire safety feature.)	
Furniture: Check the quality of the furniture, make sure there is no major damage, and that all pieces are accounted for. Make sure that any parts that fold or lift are working properly.	
Walls and ceiling: Look for apparent damage, leaks, or cracks. Examine all the seals as well as lights, vents, ducts, and fans.	
Flooring: Look for loose flooring, being sure to closely check gaps around slide outs.	
Kitchen: Open and close all cabinet doors and drawers, ensure all hardware is present, and that nothing will move during transport.	
Examine all kitchen appliances for functionality.	
Make sure there are no leaks when turning the gas on, then check all appliances that operate with propane.	

USED RV INSPECTION CHECKLIST

RV control panel: Guarantee that all indicators and functions work properly.	
MOTOR HOMES	
The Cab: Check out the steering wheel, dashboard, transmission, lights, and gauges.	
Make sure that the locks and windows are operating correctly.	
Verify that the brakes and emergency brake are working.	
MOTOR HOME ENGINE	
Check levels and potential leaks for all fluids.	
Make a visual examination for loose hoses or belts, faulty wiring, cracks, or other significant damage.	
EXTERIOR	
Windows and sidewalls: Look for cracks or discoloration and examine all the seals to make sure no moisture can enter.	
Steps and ladders: Make sure the ladder is properly secured and has no movement. Steps should be opened and closed to make sure movement is easy and secure, whether manual or motorized.	

USED RV INSPECTION CHECKLIST

Slide outs: Slide and retract any slide outs while checking for water damage and poor seals.	
Lights: You will need to connect the rig to a tow vehicle to make sure the umbilical cord functions properly. All DOT lights should function properly when activating the lights on the tow vehicle.	
Awnings and storage: Test to make sure the awning can open and close as designed, and while it's open, examine the material for any issues.	
Storage doors should be opened and closed to make sure they function properly, stay open, and lock properly.	
Check lighting, seals, and lining for damages.	
TIRES & RIMS	
Check rims, suspension, axles, brakes, and pads for proper usage from the previous owner. Anything bent or rusty deserves a closer look.	
Examine the remaining tread and PSI of the tires.	
Hitch: Look to see if all towing materials are present, in good condition, and operate smoothly.	
Stabilizer Jacks: Test to guarantee that the electronic jack system and auto-leveling feature are functioning properly.	

USED RV INSPECTION CHECKLIST

ELECTRIC	Hook up your generator if needed
Test both the AC and DC power outlets.	
Make sure all the lights in the rig are inspected.	
Make sure all the air conditioners are blowing cold air.	
Make sure all appliances are working.	
Check smoke & CO2 detectors.	
ADDITIONAL NOTES	

NOTES

CONCLUDING YOUR JOURNEY TO OFFGRID LIVING: EMBRACING THE FUTURE WITH CONFIDENCE

As you reach the final pages of the "Offgrid Planning Workbook," it's important to reflect on the journey you've embarked upon. The transition to offgrid living is a profound life choice, steeped in the pursuit of independence, sustainability, and a deeper connection with nature. The path to this unique lifestyle is as rewarding as it is challenging, and your success hinges on thorough planning, research, and a deep understanding of your own needs and aspirations.

The Importance of Thorough Planning and Research

Throughout this workbook, we've emphasized the critical role of careful planning and extensive research. Each chapter was designed to guide you through the various facets of offgrid living, from selecting the right location and building your offgrid home to managing your resources and ensuring a sustainable lifestyle. Remember, the more detailed your planning and research, the smoother your transition to offgrid living will be. It's these meticulous preparations that transform your dream into a tangible, achievable reality.

Continued Support and Resources

As you move forward, know that this workbook is just the beginning. To further assist you in your offgrid planning, we offer a range of additional resources, including comprehensive courses that delve deeper into specific aspects of offgrid living. These resources are crafted to provide you with the knowledge and skills necessary to confidently tackle each stage of your journey.

Personalized Assistance

For those who seek more personalized guidance, I offer one-on-one consulting services. This personalized approach allows me to help you tailor your offgrid plans to your unique situation, ensuring that your transition is as seamless and successful as possible. Together, we can address any specific challenges or questions you might have, bringing you closer to realizing your offgrid aspirations.

A Wish for Your Journey

As you close this workbook and look towards your future, I wish you all the best on this extraordinary journey. May the path to offgrid living bring you closer to the life you envision, filled with independence, harmony with nature, and personal fulfillment. Remember, the journey itself is just as important as the destination. Embrace each challenge, celebrate every achievement, and let your offgrid adventure unfold with joy and anticipation.

Good luck, and may your offgrid dreams flourish!

Made in the USA
Columbia, SC
20 June 2025